The Inca Ruins of Machu Picchu

Other books in the Wonders of the World series include:

WONDERS OF THE WORLD

The Inca Ruins of Machu Picchu

Jennifer Silate

KIDHAVEN PRESS
A part of Gale, Cengage Learning

GALE
CENGAGE Learning

Detroit • New York • San Francisco • New Haven, Conn • Waterville, Maine • London

© 2006 Gale, Cengage Learning

For more information, contact
KidHaven Press
27500 Drake Rd.
Farmington Hills, MI 48331-3535
Or you can visit our Internet site at gale.cengage.com

LIBRARY OF CONGRESS CATALOGING-IN-PUBLICATION DATA

Silate, Jennifer.
  Inca ruins of Machu Picchu / By Jennifer Silate.
     p. cm. — (Wonders of the world)
  Includes bibliographical references and index.
   ISBN 0-7377-3068-4 (hard cover : alk. paper)
   1. Machu Picchu Site (Peru) 2. Incas—Antiquities. 3. Incas—Social life and customs. I. Title. II. Wonders of the world (KidHaven Press)
   F3429.1.M3S55 2005
   985'.37—dc22

                                                                    2005010932

Printed in the United States of America
  5 6 7 12 11 10 09 08

CONTENTS

The Ruins the Inca Left Behind

In 1911 a young explorer named Hiram Bingham entered the mountains of Peru with a small party of men. He had studied the Inca empire, which ruled about 12 million people and controlled about 350,000 square miles (906,500 sq. km) of land in South America. The Spanish took it over in the 1500s. In his studies, Bingham learned of a lost city called Vilcabamba, where the last of the Inca had fought the Spanish. Bingham wanted to find Vilcabamba.

Bingham began his journey in Cuzco, Peru, the former capital of the Inca empire. He had the help of Sergeant Carrasco, a guard from the Cuzco government. Carrasco spoke English and Quechua, the Incan language. He helped Bingham talk with people they met along the way.

The ruins of Machu Picchu, an important city in the Inca empire, are nestled in the majestic Andes Mountains in Peru.

American archaeologist Hiram Bingham discovered the Machu Picchu ruins in 1911.

Bingham and his party walked along the old Inca roads in search of ruins. About 60 miles (97km) from Cuzco, Bingham met a man named Melchor Arteaga. Arteaga told him of ruins that could possibly be the lost city of Vilcabamba. Bingham asked Arteaga to take him there.

At ten o'clock in the morning on July 24, the men set out. Arteaga led Bingham and Carrasco to the Urubamba

River. The bridge they used to cross it was made of four logs tied together. The party had to crawl on their hands and knees to get across the river safely. After crossing the river, the men began the steep climb to the ruins. The ruins were on a **ridge** 1,500 feet (450m) above the Urubamba River, surrounded by jagged cliffs. At the end of the day, Bingham and his team finally reached the site. It was more impressive than Bingham had hoped. Walls and buildings peeked out from beneath plants and trees that had grown there in the hundreds of years since the Inca left. Despite this, Bingham could tell that they were some of the finest walls and buildings he had ever seen. The explorer was excited. He did not think that anyone would believe what he had found. He wondered if it was the lost city he had been looking for. As it turns out, the ruins were not the lost city of Vilcabamba. Instead Bingham had found Machu Picchu, a long-forgotten treasure of the Inca empire.

The Wonders of Machu Picchu

As quickly as he could, Bingham started to free the ruins from the years of tree growth that covered them. He brought in archaeology experts and local people to help him study the ruins.

During the time that Bingham spent at Machu Picchu, he uncovered some of the finest known examples of Inca architecture. Skillfully carved steps led to the ruins of homes, temples, and large buildings. Bingham could only guess what some of the buildings had been used for. Each discovery told of the skill with which the Inca

Carved stone steps at Machu Picchu lead up a walkway to a watchman's hut, also made of stone.

had built this important site. Bingham was amazed by the ruins he had found and spent about four years working to unearth them.

Carving Skills

One of the most remarkable things about Machu Picchu is its carvings. The Inca were very skilled at stone carving. Stones used to build many of the buildings at Machu Picchu were cut so masterfully that no mortar was needed to hold them in place. Most stones fit together so well that not even a credit card could fit between them.

Although the Inca only had a few different stone-carving tools, they were able to sculpt stones in many

Because the stones of this wall were so skillfully carved, no mortar was needed to hold them in place.

different ways. The stones in the walls surrounding the area called the Royal Residence were carved to look rounded and soft like pillows. In one wall, called the Artisan's Wall, stones of many different sizes and shapes make a complicated mosaic. One rock in a wall at Machu Picchu was cut so that it had 32 angles. In addition to shaping rocks to be used for building walls, the Inca also created thousands of steps at Machu Picchu. Stairways are found all over the city. They link temples, homes, and fountains. Some of the steps were expertly carved right out of hillsides from the exising rock.

The Inca used stone to create other remarkable innovations. A system of stone canals brought fresh drinking water to sixteen fountains. When Bingham discovered the system, only two areas had been damaged. Some of the fountains at Machu Picchu still work today. While the fountains provided water, other design innovations prevented too much water from entering the complex.

Other discoveries among the ruins of Machu Picchu have revealed the Inca's forethought in design construction. The Inca built drains into walls and the ground to make sure that Machu Picchu was not flooded by the more than 70 inches (178cm) of rain that fell there each year.

Agricultural Terraces

Bingham found that Machu Picchu had been divided into two sections: the Urban Sector and the Agricultural Sector. People lived in the Urban Sector, which was composed of temples, homes, and fountains. The Agricultural Sector contained **terraces** that were once used to grow crops.

Because Machu Picchu was built on a steep ridge in the Andes, terraces were used to create flat areas for farming. Terraces look like steps built of stone and soil. The Inca built hundreds of terraces at Machu Picchu. They neatly line the Agricultural Sector, which makes a

The steplike terraces of Machu Picchu were designed to create space for farming on the steep Andean ridge.

SOUTH
AMERICA
Machu
Picchu
Peru

Huayna Picchu

Temple of Three Windows

Intimachay

Intiwatana

Jail

Main
Plaza

Condor Temple
Fountains

Quarry

Main Entrance

Royal
Tomb

Royal
Residence

Temple of the Sun

stunning sight. The terraces were so well built that when Bingham reached Machu Picchu, people were still farming on some of them.

Learning from the Ruins

After Bingham finished his studies of Machu Picchu, he wrote a book describing his findings, called *Lost City of the Incas.* The book quickly became a best seller. People around the world were fascinated by what Bingham had found at Machu Picchu.

No other site from the Inca empire had such fantastic and well-preserved ruins. Because the Spanish did not find Machu Picchu when they conquered the Inca, it remained intact. Special sculpted stones that the Spanish destroyed at other Inca sites were untouched at Machu Picchu. This is why it is one of the most important archaeological sites in the world.

Because the Inca empire had no written language, archaeologists have had to use the ruins and objects the Inca left behind to learn about their culture. The ruins at Machu Picchu continue to help people today learn about the Inca way of life, although much still remains a mystery.

CHAPTER TWO

Building
Machu
Picchu

One of the mysteries of Machu Picchu is how these amazing buildings were constructed. The Inca had not discovered the wheel and had no written language. Without these tools, how did they build these complicated buildings and terraces on such a difficult piece of land? Bingham and others have worked hard to solve this mystery.

Archaeologists have learned a lot about the Inca's building techniques from places where they left construction unfinished. One unfinished building, simply called the Unfinished Temple, has a construction ramp that leads to where the Inca worked. The Inca most likely used ramps like this one to move boulders all over Machu Picchu to higher ground. In another unfinished building, the Temple of Three Windows, a large boulder sits on many smaller stones near a wall. The smaller stones probably acted as rollers to help move the large boulder. The Inca may have used this technique to move all the large rocks at Machu Picchu.

Rock Quarry

Most of the rock used to build Machu Picchu was taken from a granite rock **quarry** on the ridge. This rock quarry was probably one of the main reasons why the

The Temple of Three Windows is one of a few buildings at Machu Picchu that were never completed.

This bronze knife (left) and axe (right) are typical of the tools discovered at Machu Picchu.

Inca chose this site to build Machu Picchu. Having a quarry nearby meant that workers did not have to carry enormous boulders up the steep ridge. Instead, they could move them from the quarry to where they were needed on the ridge. This was still not an easy task, however.

Tools of the Inca

Tools found at Machu Picchu gave scientists clues to other Inca building techniques. Bronze and silver tools, shaped as axes, knives, and crowbars were left by the Inca at Machu Picchu. They also left behind hundreds of **hammerstones** which are wedge-shaped stones used to hammer rock. All these tools are a testimony to the time the Inca spent on their craft.

All the chips leftover from carving stones were put to good use. The weather at Machu Picchu is very rainy, and the area often has landslides and earthquakes. The Inca used the stone chips to build **foundations** that could withstand these natural disasters. The chips were laid deep in the ground and covered with soil. Rainwater would soak into the soil, but it would drain away through the chips. This helped to prevent landslides and is one of the main reasons why the buildings at Machu Picchu still stand today.

Farming

The same care and skill went into planning the Agricultural Sector of Machu Picchu. Hundreds of terraces cover Machu Picchu. The Inca would not have been able to farm on the land at Machu Picchu if they had not built the terraces, because the area is so steep.

The terraces were made of layers of different-size stones. The Inca placed large stones deep in the ground and covered them with smaller stones or gravel. Next the stones were covered with soil. The Incas carried the soil from the river to these terraces in baskets. The layers of stone and soil were held in place by stone walls. The foundation and stone walls supported and drained the terraces so well that they remained intact even during

The agricultural terraces and stone staircases at Machu Picchu were solidly constructed to withstand earthquakes.

earthquakes. The foundations for the terraces were similar to the foundations in the Urban Sector.

The Canal

In addition to being highly skilled builders, the Inca were also very good engineers. They built a canal to carry water from a natural spring on Machu Picchu to the Urban Sector. Scientists are amazed by the skill with which the canal was built. Today workers use special instruments to measure how steep a canal can be built. They must be steep enough for water to flow freely but not so steep that water falls out of them. The Inca did

A stone footbridge crosses the narrow canal at Machu Picchu.

This perfectly designed stone fountain is one of sixteen found throughout the Urban Sector of Machu Picchu.

not have these instruments but still managed to build a successful canal.

The canal at Machu Picchu carried about 80 gallons (303l) of water a minute from the spring. The canal is only about 5 inches (13cm) wide and 2,457 feet (749m) long. It is lined with rock and built on terraces about 7 to 20 feet (2 to 6m) high. The canal at Machu Picchu was so well built that only two areas of the canal had failed when Bingham arrived several hundred years later.

Fountains at Machu Picchu

Today the canal still brings water to sixteen fountains spread throughout the Urban Sector of Machu Picchu. The fountains are made of stone and are similarly designed. They each have a small opening for a stream of water, a rectangular basin where water can collect, and a hole in the basin for water to exit.

The fountain system was designed so that the first fountain on the canal, with the cleanest water, was near the Temple of the Sun and the Royal Residence. The Inca made sure that the emperor and the most sacred temple in Machu Picchu received the cleanest water.

Draining Machu Picchu

In addition to the deep foundations under buildings and the terraces, the Inca built drainage holes into the larger walls of Machu Picchu. The Artisan's Wall has drainage holes that were placed so that the ground floor of the rooms on one side of the wall would be cleared.

To remove the drained water from Machu Picchu, the Inca built a dry moat around the site. The moat caught the water that overflowed from the canal and the land during heavy rains.

An enormous amount of planning and skill was used to build Machu Picchu. With few tools, the Inca successfully built amazing buildings that still stand today.

CHAPTER THREE

Finding the Meaning of Machu Picchu

When Bingham first rediscovered Machu Picchu, he did not know what it was used for. Since then, archaeologists have found many clues to the site's original purpose. The first clues were in the buildings. The high level of skill used to build Machu Picchu suggests that it was built for an important purpose.

Historians ruled out Bingham's theory that Machu Picchu was the legendary Vilcabamba. The Spanish went to Vilcabamba because there are Spanish documents describing the city. The lack of Spanish **artifacts** at Machu Picchu suggests that the Spanish never found it. At other Inca sites, the presence of the Spanish invaders was very clear. Stones the Inca believed to be sacred were destroyed,

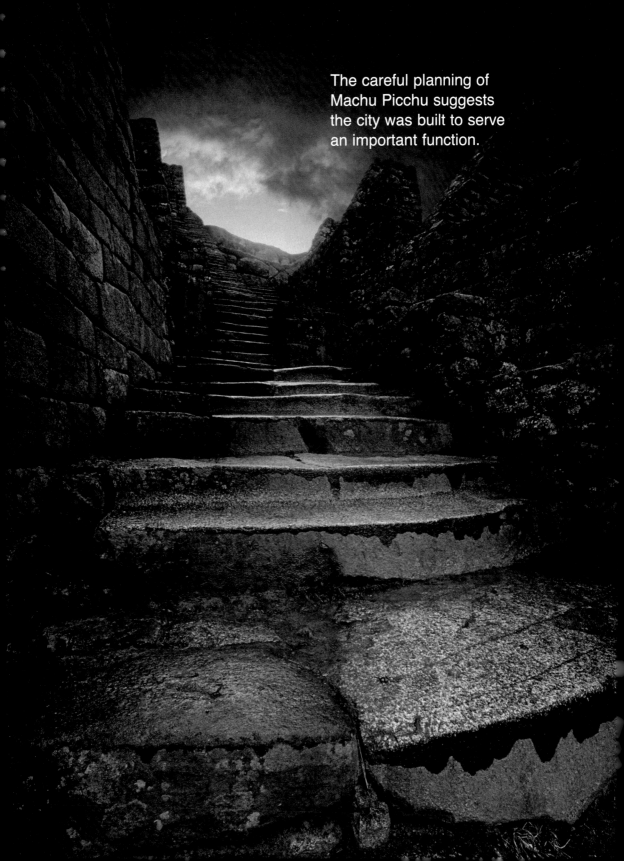

The careful planning of
Machu Picchu suggests
the city was built to serve
an important function.

and Spanish artifacts were commonly found. At Machu Picchu, there are no traces of the Spanish ever being there.

Findings also ruled out the possibility that Machu Picchu was the birthplace of the first Inca people. A scientific study of the **potsherds** found around Machu Picchu reveals that the pottery used there was made in the 1400s. This suggests that construction of Machu Picchu began in the mid-1400s, long after the first Incas had left their birthplace to take over neighboring tribes. In time, each of Bingham's guesses as to the purpose of Machu Picchu were proven wrong. Archaeologists worked to piece together the clues to find Machu Picchu's true meaning.

A Royal Retreat

A more in-depth study of Bingham's findings and those of archaeologists reveal the truth about Machu Picchu. The burial sites that Bingham and others have found gave them clues to discover Machu Picchu's purpose. Only human bones were found in most burial sites near the area. The finest grave found near Machu Picchu was for a woman who was buried with a dog, some pottery, and a few bronze artifacts. The simplicity of the graves suggests that no royal Inca were buried there. Archaeologists believe that any royal person who may have died at Machu Picchu was probably taken back to Cuzco for burial. Those who were buried near Machu Picchu were most likely artisans and servants who lived there.

In the late 1900s, historians made a discovery that helped answer many questions surrounding the purpose

Archaeologists believe Machu Picchu may have served as a royal retreat. This royal tomb is located beneath Machu Picchu's Temple of the Sun.

and meaning of Machu Picchu. They found documents regarding a court case in which descendants of the emperor Pachacuti sued for the return of a royal retreat named Picchu. Archaeologists now believe that Machu Picchu is not a city but a royal estate built by Pachacuti at the height of the Inca empire. It may have been a monument to his rule and a place to relax. The skill and care with which Machu Picchu was built may have been in tribute to Pachacuti, who was considered a creator god among the Inca.

New Studies

New studies have given archaeologists a greater understanding of the purpose of Machu Picchu. A study of the terraces have revealed that they could be used to grow enough food for only about 55 people. Experts guess that as many as 1,000 people stayed at Machu Picchu at one time. Food must have been brought to Machu Picchu from other Inca cities to feed all the visitors.

Scientists also tested the pollen at Machu Picchu to find out what kinds of plants were grown on the terraces. The results showed that corn used for food and to make tea and a drink called **chicha** and different flowers

Many of the plants and beautiful flowers of Machu Picchu are thought to have been used for ceremonial purposes.

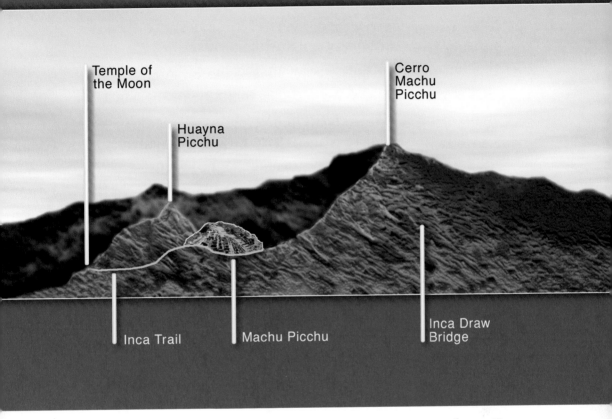

Highland Retreat

Machu Picchu sits on a mountainside high in the Andes. The site is believed to have been used by Inca royalty as a place to relax.

Temple of the Moon

Cerro Machu Picchu

Huayna Picchu

Inca Trail

Machu Picchu

Inca Draw Bridge

and herbs used to make medicines were grown there. It is thought that the plants grown at Machu Picchu were mainly used for ceremonial purposes. This adds proof to the belief that Machu Picchu was not a fully functioning city but rather a vacation spot, where it was not necessary to grow enough food for a full-time population.

Life at Machu Picchu

Historians estimate that only about 300 people lived at Machu Picchu year round. These people were from the lower classes. They had to work for the empire each year as a form of tax. They took care of the estate by tending the farms and lawns and constructing new buildings.

The emperor and other members of the royalty in the Inca empire visited Machu Picchu to escape the stresses of Cuzco and to celebrate religious events, such as the winter solstice. During this time, Machu Picchu would have been alive with activity. Goods from all over the Inca empire would have been brought here.

When the emperor and queen visited Machu Picchu, they stayed in the Royal Residence. Carefully carved stones made to look like pillows line the entranceway. The residence has several large rooms. A drain in one tells us that it was used as a bathroom. Blackened shards in another room tell us that it was used as a kitchen. The Royal Residence also has a private garden and access to the purest fountain at Machu Picchu. The emperor and his queen would have had every luxury available to an Inca and servants to provide them with whatever they needed.

A Private Temple

The emperor also had special access to the most sacred places at Machu Picchu. The Royal Residence had a private entrance into the Temple of the Sun. The emperor and other important **nobles** and priests were the only people allowed into the private temple. A ring and slots to hold a bar to lock the door are on the inside of the door. They are similar to those found on the main gate. This suggests that there was once a closeable door on the temple. In Inca times, guards most likely blocked the entrance to the temple.

Among the many buildings and temples at Machu Picchu, the Temple of the Sun was the finest. The wall that Bingham called the most beautiful in America is part of the temple. A rare indoor stairway is also used in the temple. It is expertly carved from one large stone.

The Temple of the Sun is one of the most sacred places at Machu Picchu.

Celebrations

Although many of the guests at Machu Picchu were not allowed in the Temple of the Sun, they participated in religious ceremonies in the Main Plaza. The Main Plaza is a large field in the center of the Urban Sector. Hundreds of people probably gathered there to see priests perform religious ceremonies on a ledge of the Intiwatana Pyramid, which overlooked the Main Plaza. The Intiwatana Pyramid was a very important part of Machu Picchu. It was topped with the Intiwatana stone, a four-sided stone at the highest point of Machu Picchu. Ex-

The sacred Intiwatana stone sits atop the Intiwatana pyramid near Machu Picchu's main plaza.

perts believe that the stone was probably carved to worship the surrounding mountains. We know that the stone was sacred to the Inca, but we do not know its exact purpose.

Artifacts found around Machu Picchu give us an idea of what the Inca did during these ceremonies. Potsherds with the remains of chicha on them tell us that this drink was often drunk there. Hutches built into the bottom of some walls in Machu Picchu contained the ancient droppings of guinea pigs. Roasted guinea pig is a traditional Inca delicacy and would have been served at these celebrations.

At night families probably used torchlight to help them find their way home. Historians think that rings carved into the stone walls of Machu Picchu may have held torches to light the darkened stairways. Each family at Machu Picchu had their own living area. The **elite** of Inca society were housed in the center of Machu Picchu, while farmers and workers lived along the edges of the Urban Sector. Potsherds found in a large building called a **kallanka**, also on the edge of the Urban Sector, tell us that ceremonies were held there as well. These ceremonies were most likely for the farmers and workers who lived at Machu Picchu.

Over the years much has been learned about Machu Picchu. Archaeologists have used the artifacts, skeletons, and buildings there to answer many questions about the meaning of this amazing site. Each new discovery helps us learn more about Machu Picchu and the people who lived there.

CHAPTER FOUR

Protecting and Keeping the Ruins

In the years since Bingham's rediscovery of Machu Picchu, it has become a major tourist attraction. Every year, hundreds of thousands of people travel to Machu Picchu. In 2003 about 400,000 people visited the site to experience the wonders of the ruins for themselves. Unfortunately, this large number of visitors has damaged the ruins.

Despite the care and skill the Inca used to build Machu Picchu, time has made some of the ruins unstable. In addition, the number of visitors is thought to be worsening the situation. Some experts believe that the constant pounding of feet on the ground may be one reasons why large boulders are shifting. Some tourists have directly damaged the ruins by carving their names in the stone there. In 2001 a camera crane used to film

A group of tourists appreciates the ruins of Machu Picchu from a respectful distance.

a commercial at Machu Picchu was dropped on the sacred Intiwatana stone. It left a gash about 5 inches (13cm) long. This outraged many people. In an effort to keep the most important and delicate ruins in good condition, people are no longer allowed in some of these areas.

Cable Car Controversy

Over the past several years, companies in Peru have tried to install cable cars to take visitors to Machu Picchu. This has sparked a debate between those interested in increasing tourism and those who want to limit tourism and protect the site.

Those in favor of the cable car argue that they are cleaner than the buses that currently take people to the area and would allow those who might not be able to make it up the ridge to see the amazing ruins. Some experts believe that the use of cable cars could possibly increase the number of tourists to 4,000 per day. People worry that the increase in tourism and the installation of cable car stations would destroy the important ruins. The debate continues today, and plans for building a cable car have been put on hold.

Threats to Preservation

The Inca trails that lead to Machu Picchu are also threatened by tourism. The large number of hikers who use the trails has led to litter, forest fires, and other destruction. In 2001 the Peruvian government passed regulations to limit the number of hikers on the trail to

500. They also banned hikers from walking the trails without an approved guide. In addition, each guide company is allowed to have only 40 people on the trail at one time. These restrictions, along with several others, have helped limit the destruction of Machu Picchu and the ancient Inca trails that lead to it.

In an effort to protect the Machu Picchu ruins, the Peruvian government now limits the number of visitors allowed on the trails at one time.

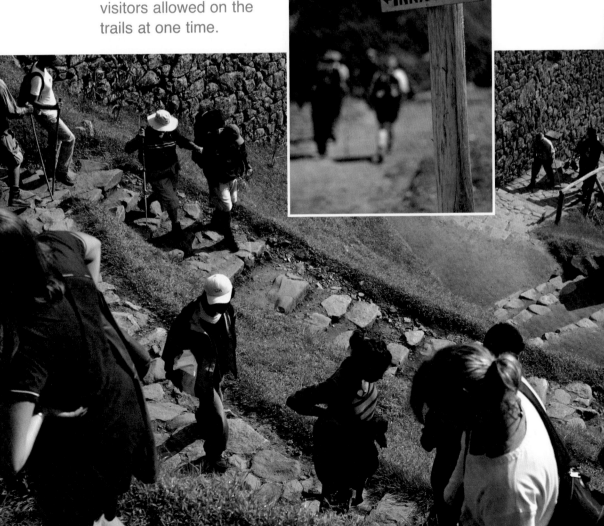

Tourists are not the only threat to Machu Picchu. Even though the Inca built Machu Picchu with amazing planning and skill, the large amount of rainfall each year slowly cuts away at the steep landscape. Earthquakes, landslides, and forest fires also threaten Machu Picchu. Landslides in the Agricultural Sector have caused some terraces to slip up to 6 feet (2m). Conservationists are working hard to restore the terraces and foundations that have slipped to keep Machu Picchu intact.

Peruvian president Alejandro Toledo (in white) visits the site of a landslide in the Machu Picchu area that killed at least six people in April 2004.

To help handle the increasing flow of tourists, a construction worker builds a new street in Machu Picchu Pueblo.

New Discoveries

Archaeologists continue to visit Machu Picchu and make new discoveries. Among some of the more recent discoveries are dozens of **obsidian** pebbles. Scientists tested the pebbles and learned that they were taken from a volcano more than 200 miles away. Archaeologists think that the pebbles had some sort of spiritual meaning because they were never shaped into tools.

While studying the soil at Machu Picchu, researchers found a single gold bracelet buried beneath a

The natural beauty of Machu Picchu and the site's many mysteries will continue to draw tourists and archaeologists for many years to come.

grassy plaza. The bracelet was found between two stones next to a buried wall. Researchers think that the bracelet may have been left beneath the stones as an offering, because it seems to have been intentionally placed where it was found. No other gold items were found at Machu Picchu. Archaeologists think that any gold that may have been there may have been given to the Spanish as ransom for a kidnapped emperor or taken when Machu Picchu was deserted.

Exciting new discoveries and the many other wonders of the Inca ruins of Machu Picchu have drawn archaeologists and others to them since their unearthing almost 100 years ago. Today archaeologists still make important discoveries that reveal more about Machu Picchu and the Inca way of life. Over the years, many of the mysteries of Machu Picchu have been solved, although some remain. While the story behind the ruins of Machu Picchu is coming to light, so much is still hidden in the dark corners of history.

Glossary

artifacts: Objects from another time or culture.

chicha: A fermented drink made from corn.

elite: A group of people thought to be better than others.

foundations: Bases or supports for buildings.

hammerstones: Stones shaped into a wedge and used as a hammer.

kallanka: A large building where group gatherings are held.

nobles: Persons of high birth or rank.

obsidian: A dark natural glass made by the cooling of lava from volcanoes.

potsherds: Pieces of pottery.

quarry: An area where there is a lot of stone.

ridge: A range of hills.

terraces: Stepped areas of flat land used for farming.

For Further Exploration

Books

Amy Allison, *Machu Picchu*. California: Lucent Books, 2003. This title from Lucent's Building History series discusses the amazing techniques the Incas used to build Machu Picchu.

Ted Lewin, *Lost City: The Discovery of Machu Picchu*. New York: Philomel, 2003. Detailed account of Hiram Bingham's famous rediscovery of Machu Picchu in 1911 with many colorful watercolor paintings.

Elizabeth Mann, *Machu Picchu: The Story of the Amazing Inkas and Their City in the Clouds*. New York: Mikaya, 2000. This book follows the rise and fall of the Inca and discusses the creation of Machu Picchu.

Fiona MacDonald, *Inca Town*. London, England: Franklin Watts, 1999. Using the city of Cuzco as a blueprint, this book details the workings and culture of an Inca town in the 15th century, the time period when Machu Picchu was being built.

Web Sites

Culture Focus (www.culturefocus.com/peru1.htm). This Web site has information and photos about the buildings, people, animals, and plants of Machu Picchu.

The Incas (http://incas.perucultural.org.pe/english). This Web site lots of information about the Inca, including their government, culture, and technologies. The text was compiled by Maria Rostworowski, a Peruvian ethnohistorian.

National Geographic: Machu Picchu (www.national geographic.com/inca/machu_picchu.html). After Bingham's rediscovery of Machu Picchu, he received money from the National Geographic Society to return and study the site more thoroughly. This Web site has some of Bingham's original pictures with information about his findings.

Index

45

Picture Credits

Cover: Corel
Anthroarcheart.org, 17, 31, 32 (main)
AP/Wide World Photos, 38, 39
© Bettmann/CORBIS, 8
© John Brecher/CORBIS, 37 (main)
Corel, 28 (both)
Getty Images, 10, 11, 25
© Wolfgang Kaehler/CORBIS, 22, 32
© Charles & Josette Lenars/CORBIS, 13 (main)
© Craig Lovell/CORBIS, 27
© Mike Maass, 20
© Northwind Picture Archive, 18 (both)
© Pilar Olivares/Reuters/Landov, 35
© Chris Rainier/CORBIS, 21
© Galen Rowell/CORBIS, 40
© James Sparshatt/CORBIS, 37 (inset)
© Brian A. Vikander/CORBIS, 7, 13 (inset)
Victor Habbick Visions, 14, 29

About the Author

Jennifer Silate is a freelance writer. She has written more than 100 nonfiction books for children. She is a member of the Society of Children's Book Writers and Illustrators. She currently lives aboard her sailboat in Maryland. This is her first book for KidHaven Press.